Animal Rights

JILLIAN POWELL

W
FRANKLIN WATTS
LONDON • SYDNEY

First published in 2009
by Franklin Watts

Copyright © Franklin Watts 2009

Franklin Watts
338 Euston Road
London NW1 3BH

Franklin Watts Australia
Level 17/207 Kent Street
Sydney, NSW 2000

Series editor: Sarah Peutrill
Editor: Sarah Ridley
Art director: Jonathan Hair
Design: www.rawshock.co.uk
Picture researcher: Diana Morris

Dewey number: 179.3

ISBN: 978 0 7496 8834 9

Printed in Malaysia

Franklin Watts is a division of Hachette
Children's Books, an Hachette UK company.
www.hachette.co.uk

Picture credits: Theo Allofs/Corbis: 17. A. Arrizurieta/AFP/Getty Images: 19t. Blue Soul Photography/Shutterstock: 14. Claver Carroll/FLPA Images: 26. Michal Cizek/AFP/Getty Images: 18. Cunningham/epa/Corbis: 5.John Daniels/Ardea: 19b. Ecoprint/Shutterstock: 7. FLPA Images: 1, 28bl. Stevens Fremont/Sygma/Corbis: 10. Philippe Hays /Rex: 6, 12. IFAW/Stewart Cook/Corbis: 15. Tea Karvinen/Rex Features: 28br. Michael Krabs/ FLPA Images: 27. Peter Lawson/Rex Features: front cover. Niderlander/Shutterstock:25. Erica Olsen/ FLPA Images: 22. William Osborn/Rex Features: 11. Bagla Palava/Sygma/Corbis: 8. Karen Pearson/ Getty Images: 23. Linda Pitkin/FLPA Images: 29. Rex Features: 9. Joel Sartore/NG/Getty Images: 13. Jerry Sharp/Shutterstock: 21. Supri/Reuters/ Corbis: 20. Charles Tayler/Shutterstock: 4. Leah-Ann Thompson/Shutterstock: 24. Penny Tweedie/ Panos: 16.

Every attempt has been made to clear copyright. Should there be any inadvertent omission please apply to the publisher for rectification.

CONTENTS

Look out for these features

A more detailed information panel.

An opportunity to get together with some friends and each take a point of view and follow it through.

An invitation to explore your own feelings.

DILEMMA
Focus on someone's difficult decision and think how you might advise them.

Look at both sides of the argument and see which you agree with.

Some topics that you could research yourself, either in the library or on the Internet.

About animal rights

We share our world with millions of different types of animal. Some animals live in the wild; others are kept on farms or live with us as pets. Since we, as humans, have rights, many people believe that the rest of the animal kingdom should have rights, too.

What are animal rights?

People argue about animal rights and what this means but most people agree that there is a right and a wrong way to treat animals. Others take this further and want animals to have similar rights to humans.

Animal rights groups

People who belong to animal rights groups fight for the rights of all animals. They run campaigns and organise protests to raise awareness and change the way animals are treated. For them, accepting that animals have rights means:

• no breeding or killing of animals for food, clothes or medicine
• no use of animals in the workplace
• no hunting
• no zoos or using animals for sport
• no experiments on animals.

A few people in animal rights groups will even use violence and break the law to achieve their aims.

Orang-utans are in danger of dying out because people have destroyed huge areas of the rainforest where they live. One of the rights most people believe in is an animal's right to live in a habitat that is natural to them.

Animal welfare

Animal welfare groups and charities believe animals can be used for food, clothing and medical research as long as they are well cared for. They campaign to protect animals from cruelty. They raise funds to educate people about animal welfare in general, and in farming. They rescue animals that have been badly treated, neglected or abandoned. The most famous animal welfare group is the RSPCA.

YOUR CALL Do you think animals should have the same rights as humans? Are there any times when you would break the law to protect an animal?

IN FOCUS

Greenpeace

This international organisation campaigns on conservation issues. As part of this, Greenpeace takes direct action to stop endangered whales from being hunted. Greenpeace members drive inflatable boats between whales and whaling ships and use high-power water pumps to hide the whales from the harpooners. This can result in activists being arrested and charged with breaking the law.

A Greenpeace dinghy disrupts the work of a Japanese whaling ship to protect whales.

Eating animals

Animal rights campaigners believe that animals have the right to life. Many of them follow a strict vegetarian diet. However, for millions of years people have eaten meat.

These sheep are being taken to market. Many meat-eaters do not like to think about the way animals are farmed and sent to slaughter.

Vegetarians

Some people believe it is wrong to kill animals for food. They become vegetarian and do not eat meat, poultry or fish. Vegans follow a similar diet but cut out eggs and dairy products as well. They believe that animals have as much right to life as people.

Natural meat-eaters

Naturally, people are omnivores. Our bodies are designed to eat a mixed diet that includes meat or fish, fruit and vegetables, cereals, grains and seeds. It can be argued that eating meat is the easiest way to have a balanced diet although some people eat too much meat, and risk damaging their health as a result.

RESEARCH IT YOURSELF

Find out about vegetarian and vegan lifestyles. Check out www.youngveggie.org, a website aimed at young vegetarians.

Scientists are experimenting with growing meat from cells in a laboratory. This would end the need for rearing animals for food. Would you eat products like this if it meant no more animals were killed for food?

ARGUMENTS FOR AND AGAINST EATING ANIMALS AS FOOD

FOR!

- Meat provides protein and other important nutrients for human health.
- Animals hunt down and eat other animals anyway.
- Many animals would have no purpose without farming.
- We are natural omnivores — our bodies can digest many different types of food, including meat. It is our natural diet.
- Animals can be farmed kindly.

AGAINST!

- Animals have the right to life and should not be killed for their meat.
- A vegetarian diet is healthier as it is lower in fat.
- Some types of livestock farming are cruel.
- If everyone became vegetarian, it would be easier to feed the world's population.
- Sheep and cows produce methane, a greenhouse gas.

Cows produce a greenhouse gas called methane when they digest grass. This gas contributes to climate change.

Wearing fur

Traditionally, animals have been trapped or hunted for their fur or skin. The first clothes and blankets used by man were made from animal skins. Today, hunters continue to kill animals for their skins, but others farm them — something that upsets many people.

Anti-fur campaigns

Animal rights activists and many other people say it is wrong to kill animals for their skins. Most fur comes from farmed animals, many of which have spent their lives in small cramped cages. The rest comes from wild animals and, despite laws to prevent this, endangered animals are killed for their skins. In addition, there is no need for people to wear fur to stay warm since there are plenty of modern fabrics that work just as well.

IN FOCUS

Fur trade

The International Fur Trade Federation works to ensure that farmed animals are well cared for and that endangered animals are not killed for their skins. Animals that are most commonly used to make clothes include: foxes, sheep, beavers, minks, raccoons, chinchillas, cats, dogs, seals, coyote and hamsters.

Mink farms

Mink is the animal most commonly farmed for its fur. In the wild, mink spend some of their lives swimming, something they cannot do on a fur farm. Mink that escape from fur farms into the wild cause a problem as they eat other wildlife.

Fur lovers

Supporters of the fur trade say that people have worn animal skins for thousands of years and should be allowed to continue doing so. They argue that most fur comes from fur farms, and that fur farmers have to follow strict rules about the way they

An Indian officer guards tiger skins, discovered in a raid on poachers.

care for the animals. Others say it is all right to wear fur provided it is not farmed, and that most animals killed for their skins are not endangered. They argue that many people who object to fur wear leather, which is no different.

Some fashion designers continue to use real fur, as shown by this model's hat.

ARGUMENTS FOR AND AGAINST THE FUR TRADE:

FOR!

- People have worn animal skins for thousands of years.
- Animals are killed for food so why not for fur?
- There are laws and rules to protect animals on fur farms.
- People have the right to wear fur.
- Wearing fur is no different from wearing leather.

AGAINST!

- It is wrong to kill animals.
- Fur farming is cruel.
- Existing laws do not stop cruelty on fur farms.
- Fake fur is just as good.
- Endangered animals continue to be killed for their skins.

YOUR CALL Some people think it is okay to wear old furs as long as you don't buy new. But others think wearing any real fur is wrong and encourages the fur trade. What do you think?

RESEARCH IT YOURSELF

Find out about the leather industry.
Where do the animal skins come from to make leather? Check out the education pages on www.all-about-leather.co.uk.

Farm animals

Farm animals are reared to provide people with meat, dairy products, eggs and wool. Cows, sheep, pigs, goats, fish, chickens and camels are a few of the many animals farmed throughout the world.

Livestock farming

People have farmed animals for thousands of years, but does that make it right? Animal rights activists think that farming animals for food is wrong because animals have the right to life. In addition, several top scientists advise that people should eat less meat in order to reduce the amount of livestock farming worldwide. This is because livestock farming contributes to climate change. Rainforests, which help to combat climate change, are cut down for cattle farming. Sheep and cows produce methane, a greenhouse gas, when they digest food.

Welfare in farming

Animal welfare groups believe animal welfare should be the most important concern in farming today. They say that

These pigs will live out their lives in an indoor pig unit. Free range pigs would live in a field, or be able to go outside for part of the day.

animals reared on intensive farms live short, miserable lives. Free range and organically farmed animals lead more natural lives. By reading food labels, shoppers can choose to buy meat from these animals, although it is usually more expensive.

Free range chickens get more space to move about than those that are farmed intensively.

ROLE-PLAY: CULTURE CLASH

These two people disagree about the rights and wrongs of factory-farmed chickens. Can you add to their arguments?

1

"It is cruel keeping birds in crowded barns. They can suffer stress and leg problems because they gain weight so fast. We should all be prepared to pay more for free range poultry."

Animal welfare officer, Jane Sheena

2

"I am a single mother and I just can't afford to buy free range chicken. My priority is to feed my family on the money I have each week."

Mother, Tara Wilson

RESEARCH IT YOURSELF

Find out about some of the other issues surrounding livestock farming.
Investigate the veal trade, battery chicken farming or fish farming. You could look at www.chickenout.tv — the website for the Chicken Out Campaign for free range poultry farming.

IN FOCUS

Foie gras
Foie gras is a rich paté made from the liver of a duck or a goose that has been fattened up by force-feeding. Most are kept in small cages and fed until their livers are ten times the normal size, causing problems with breathing and walking. Food lovers enjoy the special flavour of this expensive food product but some meat-eaters refuse to eat it, because of the way it is produced.

Hunting and fishing

In the past, people hunted and fished for survival. They needed the meat to eat and the skins for warmth. Today, hunting, shooting and fishing is a subject that raises strong feelings on both sides.

For many years, anti-hunt activists in the UK disrupted hunts and demanded a change to the law, which has now happened. The hunting of wild mammals with dogs is now an offence.

Against hunting

Animal rights activists believe that it is wrong to kill animals, especially for sport. They also think it is cruel to make animals suffer stress or injury in the name of sport. Many want to see all hunting, fishing and shooting banned. They educate people about why hunting is wrong and cruel by making films, writing newpaper articles, disrupting hunts and campaigning for changes to hunting and shooting laws.

Pro-hunting

Traditionally, hunting has been accepted in the countryside or the wilderness. It provides food, animal skins and jobs for people, often in areas where there are few jobs available. Some research shows that hunting controls animal pests in a less cruel way than other forms of pest control, such as poison or traps.

Breeding for hunting

Recently hundreds of ranches in the USA have begun to breed unusual animals for hunting. People will pay thousands of dollars to shoot zebra, antelope or even endangered oryx. Some of the profit from the hunting goes to animal conservation. The ranchers argue that breeding animals for hunting is no different from breeding them for food.

Inuit hunters have killed this caribou for food. Other hunters enjoy hunting for pleasure.

IN FOCUS

Traditional Chinese medicine

Some traditional Chinese medicines contain animal parts. Tigers, rhinos and seahorses are all illegally hunted and sold to the makers of these medicines, even though there are international laws to protect them.

ROLE PLAY: CULTURE CLASH

Here are two views on blood sports. Try arguing out the debate with a friend.

1 "It is wrong to kill animals for sport. Hunting causes animals fear and pain. If people want sport there are alternatives like clay shooting and drag hunting which don't harm animals."

Student, Jason Holt

2 "Hunting and shooting are part of country life. They provide jobs for local people and help to control the animals that are pests to farmers."

Gamekeeper, Jim Bland

Culling

Culling means reducing the number of animals in a population by killing some of them. It can also mean killing animals that are sick or weak in a herd or flock. Animals are culled for different reasons all over the world.

Culling for the greater good

In some places, people cull animals to protect food stocks or livelihoods. Deer and elephants can destroy farmers' crops in Africa or India, and seals eat fish stocks and make holes in fishermen's nets. Animals can also spread disease. Badgers have been blamed for causing tuberculosis in British cattle, and birds spread the avian flu virus. People in favour of culling also say it stops animal populations from growing too big, and helps keep the remaining animals healthy.

Culling is murder

If you believe that people do not have the right to kill animals, then culling is completely unacceptable. People concerned with animal welfare are worried by the cruel methods used to cull some animals. Seals are culled in some areas as they eat a lot of fish. The seal pups are clubbed to death using big sticks or ice picks. There are alternatives to culling seals, such as noise devices that scare seals away from fishing nets. Some problem animals could be moved to different habitats, or their food source could be limited to reduce numbers.

Kangaroos are culled in Australia when their numbers grow too big. They can become pests, eating crops and grazing land.

ARGUMENTS FOR AND AGAINST CULLING

FOR!

- To protect another species.
- To protect people's ways of making a living.
- To stop animals eating food sources.
- To stop herds or flocks becoming too big.
- To keep surviving animals fit and strong.

AGAINST!

- Animals have the right to life and we do not have the right to kill them.
- Culling can be cruel.
- There are alternatives to culling.
- Animals will increase after culling anyway.
- Flocks or herds may control their own numbers by reducing the birth rate.

RESEARCH IT YOURSELF

Find out why the Canadian government allows so many seals to be culled every year. Check out information from Fisheries and Oceans Canada, www.dfo-mpo.gc.ca, and the marine wildlife conservation organisation, www.seashepherd.org.

YOUR CALL Should animals be culled if they are doing harm to other animal groups? Do you think we have the right to decide?

Every year seals are culled in Canada, to control the seal population. Shocking images, such as this, fuel the campaign against culling.

Working animals

Animals are used by people in many areas of work, from farming and transport to tourism and police work. They also play an important role in search and rescue, security and as helpers to people who have lost their sight or hearing.

Working animals

In the past, farmers used animals to pull machinery and carts. In poorer countries, this continues. Horses, oxen, buffaloes and bullocks work alongside farmers in the fields. Donkeys and mules carry heavy loads and work mills and wells. Sometimes working animals are ill-treated or overworked. Animal welfare campaigners say there should be stricter laws to protect working animals.

Pack animals, such as donkeys, are used to carry heavy loads to market.

IN FOCUS
Hard-working donkeys

Worldwide, millions of donkeys are used to pull farm machinery or carry heavy loads. Although many families depend on their donkey to help them earn money or collect vital firewood, they cannot always afford to care for the donkey or allow it enough rest. Charities, such as The Donkey Sanctuary, set up vet clinics and give out advice to help people care for working donkeys.

Tourists enjoy an elephant safari. Elephants move very quietly, allowing the tourists to get close to other wildlife.

? Dilemma:

Josh is going on holiday with his parents. There will be the opportunity to go on an elephant safari. The brochure says that the elephants are well cared for and that the experience is unmissable but Josh has heard that elephants are often overworked and treated unkindly by their trainers. What should he do?

Tourism

Elephant safaris, camel rides and trips in a pony trap encourage tourism and provide jobs. It is said that close contact with the animals can help raise awareness of conservation issues. But is it cruel to keep these animals in captivity and force them to work? Many of the animals work long hours and do not always get enough rest, food or water. Elephants are used in Asia and Africa to carry tourists up a hill, or on safari. Some of their trainers use sticks, hooks or chains to keep them under control, and elephants can suffer skin and eye problems, as well as blistered feet.

RESEARCH IT YOURSELF

Find out about working dogs. Use the Internet or the library to learn more about sheep dogs, guide dogs, sniffer dogs, police dogs and search and rescue dogs. Check out websites like www.guidedogs.org.uk and www.nsarda.org.uk.

Sporting and circus animals

 Some animals are trained to entertain us. They perform on the street, at the circus or at race events. Other spectator events include dog fights, even though they are against the law, and bull fights, which are legal in Spain.

Happy performers?

Most owners and trainers want their animals to be in good health so that they will perform well at the circus or on the racetrack. Many rely on the animals to make money for them — it is their job. Animals form close bonds with their trainers and seem to enjoy taking part in sports or shows.

Forced to perform?

Should animals perform for our entertainment? Some believe it is cruel to force animals to race and risk injury in the process. Circus life is not right for an animal as they are constantly travelling, often in cramped conditions. They suffer stress from the training, the crowds and the loud noises. Many people think bull fighting should be banned, as the bull suffers in the bull ring and meets a painful death.

Horses and their jockeys clear a jump. It takes a lot of money and time to keep a racehorse in top condition.

In a bull fight, the matador creates a show as he slowly angers the bull and finally kills him.

? **Dilemma:**

When Jane goes to stay with a Spanish family on a school exchange, they want to take her to see a bull fight. But Jane is an animal lover and can't bear the idea of it. Should she go or refuse the invitation and risk upsetting her hosts?

Greyhound racing

Animal welfare groups have called for greyhound racing to be banned. Each year, thousands of greyhounds are culled when they become too old to race, are injured or do not look as if they will become good racers. There are charities that rescue greyhounds but many dogs just 'disappear'.

Greyhounds are usually between 18 months and 4 years old when they are retired from racing.

Zoos and safari parks

Z oos and safari parks are public places where people can see animals in captivity. Most animals in zoos and safari parks are born through captive breeding programmes or have come from other zoos.

Zoos and conservation

Zoos and safari parks play an important role in conservation. They run breeding programmes that increase the numbers of endangered species. Scientists are able to carry out research on animal care and behaviour. In the meantime, visitors learn about animals, and may come to care more deeply about preserving them in the wild.

Captive breeding programmes

These programmes can help endangered species survive. In some cases, animals bred in this way have been released into the wild although this is difficult, as the animals have been reared away from their natural prey and predators. The other problem is that breeding from small populations could affect the health of the baby animals.

This tiger has successfully given birth to cubs at a zoo.

It can be upsetting to see a large animal behind bars.

FOR!

- They teach us about animals and animal conservation.
- Breeding programmes can protect endangered species.
- They provide scientists with the chance to study wild animals.
- They provide good diets and veterinary care.
- Some are large and animals can roam freely.

AGAINST!

- It is wrong to keep animals in captivity.
- Animals have the right to live in their natural habitat.
- It is cruel to keep animals in small cages.
- Captive breeding programmes rarely return any animals to the wild.
- Animals can show signs of stress and unhappiness and some may die earlier than they would in the wild.

The problem with zoos and safari parks

As far as animal rights supporters are concerned, it is unacceptable to keep animals in captivity. For others, it is more of a welfare issue. Many zoos have restricted space and struggle to provide the animals with a suitable living space. Zoo animals can suffer unhappiness or stress as they are unable to follow a natural lifestyle. A recent study found that the average lifespan of African elephants in zoos was only 19 years compared with 56 years in the wild. Safari parks have more space but the animals are still on show for several hours a day. Some people think it is wrong to display animals for our amusement and education.

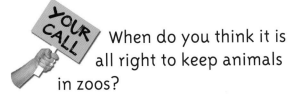
YOUR CALL When do you think it is all right to keep animals in zoos?

Pets

Many kinds of animals are kept as pets. Dogs, cats, rabbits, hamsters and fish are among the most popular pets, but some people keep unusual or exotic pets including snakes, terrapins, sugar gliders and spiders.

Some people over-feed their pet so that the animal becomes obese.

Lifelong care

Pets need to be looked after for the whole of their natural lives. In particular they need:

• a home that is kept clean and is suitable for their size and needs
• a healthy diet and fresh water
• freedom to exercise
• companionship from people or from another animal
• treatment and health care, as required.

People can use different methods to train and discipline their pets. Collars which give a small electric shock are sometimes used to train dogs that are behaving badly. But some people think they are cruel and there are better alternative methods for training. On some issues, animal welfare groups can clash with pedigree breeders on what is right or wrong.

IN FOCUS

Animal welfare laws

In the UK and elsewhere, there are rules concerning the fair treatment of pets. Cruel or neglectful owners can be taken to court, fined and even sent to prison for treating pets badly.

Suitable pets

People enjoy keeping a pet — it gives them an interest as well as companionship. However, choosing a pet involves careful thought. Reptiles, for instance, are exotic and unusual pets, but it can be difficult and expensive to care for them properly. Birds need space to fly in and follow their natural behaviour. Many pets end up in rescue centres, in need of a new home. If you are thinking of getting a new pet, you could start by asking a local rescue centre if they have something suitable.

Iguanas grow to 1.5 metres in length. Pet owners need to be prepared to care for such a large animal.

ROLE-PLAY: CLASSROOM PETS

Here are two opinions on keeping classroom pets. Can you take one of the arguments and follow it through?

1 "The classroom is no place for a pet. Classrooms can be noisy places and animals can get scared if they are handled too much or feel lonely if they are left for long periods."

Animal lover, Jack Robbins

2 "Keeping a classroom pet helps to teach children about animals and how to care for them. It can be really good for children who don't have pets at home."

Teacher, Laura Walters

? **Dilemma:**
Rachel's cat Kandy is 17 years old, but lately she has been ill. Now the vet has told Rachel that Kandy is in pain and she should not be allowed to suffer any longer. Rachel can't bear the idea of losing Kandy but the vet says it would be the kindest thing for the cat. What should she do?

Animal research

Scientists use animals to test new products and develop new drugs to see if they are safe for people to use. They also investigate how animals' bodies work to improve the health of animals and humans.

Life-saving research

Animal research has helped develop thousands of medical treatments used in medicine today, from antibiotics to life-saving operations. For many scientists, the discoveries that result from the experiments make up for any suffering caused to the animals. Research scientists take care that animals do not suffer unnecessarily.

IN FOCUS

Drug tests

New medical drugs have to be tested to make sure they are completely safe. There are several stages:

1. The drug is tested using computer models and human cells grown in a laboratory.
2. If the drug passes stage 1, it is tested on animals. Scientists carefully watch the animals for side-effects.
3. If the drug passes stage 2, it is tested on healthy people. Finally, the drug is tested on people who are ill.

Against animal experiments

Thousands of animals live out their lives in research laboratories. Laws protect them from cruel treatment, but they still spend their lives in cramped cages and can suffer stress and pain during experiments. Since animals are different from people, the results of the

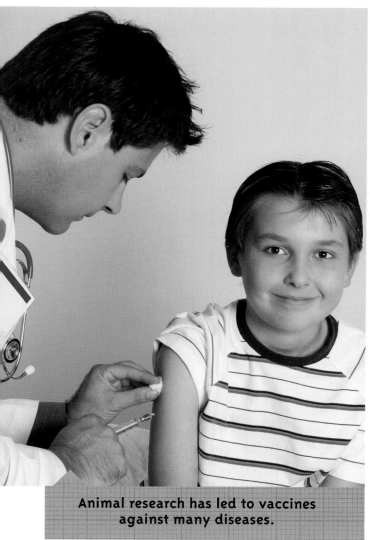

Animal research has led to vaccines against many diseases.

Thousands of animals, including these mice, are bred for animal testing each year.

experiments can be unreliable. Some people say all animal testing is wrong while others think it should only be used when there are no alternatives.

? Dilemma:

Jodie's dad has heart disease and he could be helped by an operation. The surgeon has said he will replace a heart valve with one from a pig. Jodie is an animal rights campaigner and her parents are worried about telling her the truth. What should they do?

ARGUMENTS FOR AND AGAINST ANIMAL TESTING

FOR!

- Animal testing has helped to develop vaccines against diseases like measles, mumps and rabies.
- Cancer drugs rely on animal testing.
- Operations on animals help to develop surgery techniques.
- The law protects animals from cruelty or bad treatment.
- Millions of animals are killed for food every year.

AGAINST!

- Animals have a right to life.
- Testing drugs on animals is unreliable as they can react differently from people.
- There are alternatives such as computer models, statistics and test tube studies on human tissue.
- Strict laws have not stopped some researchers treating animals cruelly.
- Animal stress can make the results of experiments unreliable.

 What do you think about testing drugs on animals? Do you think you would feel differently if you suffered from a disease that cannot be cured currently?

Breeding and pedigree

Breeders can change the way animals look and behave. They carefully choose which animals they will allow to breed in order to get particular results — bigger animals, more healthy animals, animals of a particular colour. The list is endless.

Merino sheep have been bred to produce the maximum amount of wool on their wrinkly skins.

Farming

Since ancient times, farmers have bred animals to improve them for their own use. So if a farmer wanted bigger pigs, he would try to get his biggest pigs to breed, in the hope of larger piglets. Farmers still take care when they are breeding their animals. Prize rams, bulls or boars are treasured. In addition, farmers can now use artificial insemination to ensure that all the cows, for instance, produce offspring of a particular bull.

Pedigree pets

A pedigree is simply a record of the parents, grandparents and so on of an animal. Dogs and cats have been bred for all sorts of different characteristics. Pedigree breeds have to meet certain standards, such as short legs for a dachshund. Over the last 100 years, dachshunds have been bred to have shorter and shorter legs. The better the pedigree of an animal, the more valuable it is, and the more likely it is to win prizes at shows.

Inter-breeding

Sometimes, as a result of breeding animals that are closely related, animals develop health problems affecting breathing, joints or even brains. Some breeders cull animals that don't meet breed standards. Most animal breeders want healthy animals above all else, but some breeders lose sight of this.

What do you think about pedigree breeds? Do you think it is all right that people can breed animals to look a certain way, even if it might cause them health problems?

RESEARCH IT YOURSELF

Find out more about pedigree dog breeds and the standards set for each breed. Check out www.thekennelclub.org.uk

Many pugs (below) suffer from breathing problems caused by being bred to look the way they do.

Endangered animals

Thousands of animal species are endangered. This means that there are so few of them left on the planet that they could die out altogether in the wild. The world has already lost thousands of species, including mammals, bird and insects.

The road to extinction

Animals become endangered when their habitat is destroyed or damaged. Loss of habitat means less food and destroys the natural way of life. Gradually certain types of animal reduce in number until there are so few left that they die out altogether. It is usually people who destroy habitats by clearing land for houses, roads or farming or by producing pollution through car use and industry. Hunters and poachers have hunted some animals to extinction.

Climate change

Climate change threatens many animal species, including humans. If the planet warms and seasons change, this will affect food supplies and habitats. Climate change is occurring because of the greenhouse effect. Gases, many of which are produced by car engines and the burning of oil and coal, collect in the atmosphere, trapping heat, rather than allowing it to escape into space.

Thousands of types of butterfly are struggling to survive, including this mazarine blue butterfly.

Polar bears hunt seals and other prey from sea ice. If global warming causes the sea ice to melt, polar bears may die out.

Hawksbill turtles are hunted for their meat and beautiful shells.

IN FOCUS

Turtles

Humans are the main threat to turtles. Turtles can mistake plastic bags for jellyfish, eat them and then starve to death as a result. People steal turtle eggs for food, hunt them for their shells, destroy their nesting sites by building hotels on the beach and trap them in fishing nets.

Protecting animals

Animal rights and welfare groups both campaign to protect endangered species but they can disagree on some issues, such as captive breeding programmes in zoos. International laws protect some endangered species, such as whales. But many types of whale remain endangered because people find ways around the rules. Even though large scale whaling was banned in 1986, whalers in countries such as Japan and Iceland still kill whales for 'scientific research'. Governments and organisations continue to work towards protecting endangered wildlife and their habitats.

YOUR CALL

Elephants are an endangered species so there are laws to protect them. But elephants can sometimes destroy crops, raid grain stores and even kill people in rural communities in Africa and Asia. How can both be protected?

Glossary

Activists	People who take action on something they believe in.
Animal welfare	The well-being of animals.
Antibiotics	Drugs that fight infections caused by bacteria.
Artificial insemination	Fertilising a female using sperm taken from a male.
Breeding programme	Mating animals to increase their numbers.
Campaign	Organised action to achieve specific aims.
Climate change	Gradual change in the Earth's climate and weather patterns; currently a gradual warming of the Earth's climate.
Computer model	A program on a computer that uses data to make forecasts.
Conservation Issues	Subjects to do with protecting and preserving.
Culling	Reducing numbers by removing some animals.
Endangered	Threatened with becoming extinct.
Extinct	Died out.
Factory-farming	Method of farming intensively to achieve maximum profit.
Food stocks	Supplies of a food source.
Free range	Method of farming that rears animals partly outdoors with freedom to roam.
Habitat	Natural surroundings where plants or animals live.
Intensive farming	A method of farming using pesticides and indoor livestock units to maximise production.
Livestock	Farm or ranch animals.
Methane	A colourless gas believed to contribute to climate change.
Mules	Animals that are a cross between a horse and a donkey.
Nutrients	Goodness found in food.
Obese	Clinically overweight.
Omnivore	An animal that eats all kinds of foods including meat.
Organic	Using a method that avoids the use of chemicals.
Pesticides	Chemicals used in farming to prevent pests attacking crops.
Poacher	Someone who hunts fish or game illegally.
Predators	Animals that hunt others for food.
Prey	Animals hunted as food.
Rights	Basic needs and expectations.
Side-effects	Effects not originally intended.
Stress	Feeling of worry because of fear or pain.
Vaccines	Injections of substances that protect against diseases.
Vegetarian	Someone who eats no meat, poultry or fish.
Vegan	Someone whose diet is based on plant foods.
Wilderness	Wild and uninhabited place.

Further information

Websites

www.animalaid.org.uk
The website for the UK's largest animal rights group.

www.bluecross.org.uk
The website for charity that campaigns for the welfare of the UK's pets.

www.bret.org.uk
A charity who provides secondary schools with speakers and information leaflets, videos etc about the humane and responsible use of animals in medical research.

www.league.org.uk
The website for the campaign against cruel sports.

www.rspca.org.uk
The website for the leading charity that campaigns for the welfare of animals around the world.

www.rspca.org.au
The website for the RSPCA in Australia.

www.americananimalwelfare.com
The website of an organisation that campaigns for the welfare of animals in America.

Note to parents and teachers: Every effort has been made by the Publishers to ensure that these websites are suitable for children, that they are of the highest educational value, and that they contain no inappropriate or offensive material. However, because of the nature of the Internet, it is impossible to guarantee that the contents of these sites will not be altered. We strongly advise that Internet access is supervised by a responsible adult.

Index

These are the lists of contents for each title in *Your Call:*

Alcohol

What is alcohol? • What happens when you drink alcohol? • Alcohol in everyday life • Social drinking • Learning to drink • Under-age drinking • Binge drinking • Alcohol and health • Addicted to alcohol • Alcohol and the law • Drink-driving • Alcohol and violence • Alcohol in different cultures

Animal Rights

About animal rights • Eating animals • Wearing fur • Farm animals • Hunting and fishing • Culling • Working animals • Sporting and circus animals • Zoos and safari parks • Pets • Animal research • Breeding and pedigree • Endangered animals

Being A Vegetarian

What is a vegetarian? • What is a vegan? • Animal welfare • Green vegetarians • Feeding the world • The healthy choice? • A balanced diet Vegetarian children • Read the label • Going vegetarian • Clothes and make-up • Extreme vegetarians • Vegetarianism around the world

Bullying

What is bullying? • Why do people bully? • Emotional bullying • Verbal bullying • Physical bullying • Cyber bullying • Racist bullying • Bullying at home • Bullying at school • Bullying in sport • Stop the bullying! • Being a witness • Anti-bullying groups

Campaigning for Change

Why do people campaign for change? • Lobbying and pressure groups • Demonstrations, marches and rallies • Publicity stunts • Big events • Charities • Media campaigns • Local campaigns • Raising awareness • Campaign labels and marks • Modern technology • Extremists • Getting involved

Gangs

About gangs • Why people join gangs • Looking alike • Group behaviour • Peaceful gangs • Violent gangs • Girl gangs • Turf wars • Knife crimes • Gun crimes • Social crimes • Safer streets • Youth projects